D1625178

dreams

dreams

A Book of Symbols

Illustrated by Haydn Cornner

RUNNING PRESS
PHILADELPHIA • LONDON

Library of Congress Cataloging-in-Publication Number 97-66828

ISBN 0-7624-0253-9

This book may be ordered by mail from the publisher.
Please include $1.00 for postage and handling.
But try your bookstore first!

Running Press Book Publishers
125 South Twenty-second Street
Philadelphia, Pennsylvania 19103-4399

introduction

> "If the gods love men
> they will certainly disclose their
> purposes to them in sleep."
>
> **CICERO**

For ages, philosophers, prophets, and statesmen have been fascinated by the ability of dreams to explain experiences. Death, famine, and chance happenings have been predicted and sometimes prevented because people have always been aware of the importance of subconscious messages.

Almost a century ago, Gustavus Hindman Miller compiled 10,000 dream symbols and their meanings in an effort to help further the human ability to decipher hidden meanings in dreams. He believed that, if correctly interpreted, dreams could be important sources of information about the future, the present, the past, and the subconscious mind. The symbols presented in this book are excerpted from Miller's work and will help you unlock the mysteries of your dreams.

Learn about your love life by dreaming of a candle, a fawn, or the moon. Let a mountain—or your own nose—guide your business affairs. Discover the prophetic power of onions, potatoes, and apples while finding out what bicycles and butterflies foretell.

Let Dreams be your guide to understanding these and many other dream symbols.

acorn

Seeing acorns in a dream predicts pleasant things ahead and that much gain is to be expected. To pick them from the ground foretells success after weary labors. For a woman to eat them denotes that she will rise from a station of labor to a position of ease and pleasure. To shake them from trees denotes that you will rapidly attain your wishes in business or love.

angels

When wicked people dream of angels it is a demand to repent; to good people it should be a consolation. If the dream is unusually pleasing, you will hear of the health of friends and receive a legacy from an unknown relative.

apples

To see red apples on trees with green foliage is exceedingly fortunate to the dreamer. Ripe apples denote that the time has arrived for you to realize your hopes. Think over what you intend to do and go fearlessly ahead. A ripe apple on top of a tree warns you not to aim too high.

arrow

Pleasure follows
this dream.
Entertainments,
festivals, and
pleasant journeys
may be expected.
Suffering will
cease.

bear

A bear signifies overwhelming competition in pursuits of every kind. To kill a bear foretells liberation from former entanglements.

bed

A clean, white bed denotes a peaceful end of worries. If a woman dreams of making a bed, a new lover and pleasant occupation are imminent. To dream that you are sleeping on a bed in the open air foretells that you will have delightful experiences and opportunity for improving your future.

bicycle

To dream of riding a
bicycle uphill signifies
bright prospects.
Riding downhill calls
for care—misfortune
hovers near.

birthday gifts

Receiving happy surprises signifies many high accomplishments. Working people will advance in their trade.

butterfly

To see a butterfly among flowers and green grasses indicates prosperity and fair attainments. To see butterflies flying about denotes news from absent friends by letter or from someone who has seen them.

candy

To dream of making candy denotes profit accruing from industry. To dream of eating crisp, new candy implies social pleasures and much lovemaking among the young and old.

candles

To see candles burning with a clear and steady flame denotes the constancy of those around you and a well-grounded fortune. For a maiden to dream that she is molding candles indicates that she will have an unexpected offer of marriage and a pleasant visit to distant relatives. If she is lighting a candle, she will meet her lover clandestinely because of parental objections.

cherubs

To dream of cherubs foretells that you will have some distinct joy which will leave an impression of lasting good upon your life.

crown

To dream of a crown predicts a change of mode in the habit of one's life. The dreamer will travel a long distance from home and form new relations. To dream of crowning a person shows your own worthiness.

dance

To dream of seeing a crowd of merry children dancing signifies loving, obedient, and intelligent children and a cheerful and comfortable home. To young people it denotes easy tasks and many pleasures. To see older people dancing foretells a brighter outlook for business. To dream that you are dancing means that some unexpected good fortune will come to you.

daybreak

To watch the day break in a dream is an omen of successful undertakings. But if the scene is indistinct and weird, it may imply disappointment when success in business or love seems assured.

diamonds

To dream of owning diamonds is a
very promising dream signifying great
honor and recognition from high
places. Diamonds are omens of good
luck, unless stolen from the bodies of
dead persons. If that occurs, they
foretell that your own unfaithfulness
will be discovered by your friends.

ducks

To dream of seeing wild ducks on a clear stream of water signifies fortunate journeys, perhaps across the sea. To see ducks flying foretells a brighter future for you. It also denotes marriage and children in a new home.

dynamite

To see dynamite in a dream is a sign of approaching change and the expanding of one's affairs.

eagles

To see an eagle soaring above you denotes lofty ambitions which you will struggle fiercely to realize; nevertheless, you will gain your desires. To see an eagle perched on distant heights predicts that you will possess fame, wealth, and the highest position available in your country.

earrings

To see earrings in
dreams is an omen
that good news
and interesting work
are before you.

elephants

To dream of riding an elephant denotes that you will possess wealth and honors which you will wear with dignity. You will rule absolutely in business affairs and your word will be law in the home. Many elephants denote prosperity. One lone elephant signifies that you will live in a small but solid way. Feeding an elephant foretells that you will elevate yourself in your community by your kindness.

evergreen

This dream brings boundless resources of wealth, happiness, and learning. It is an indication of future prosperity.

fawn

To dream of seeing a fawn denotes that you will have true and upright friends. To the young it indicates faithfulness in love.

feathers

To dream of seeing feathers falling around you denotes that your burden in life will be light and easily borne. To see eagle feathers predicts that your aspirations will be realized. To see chicken feathers denotes small annoyances.

fingers

To see beautiful hands with white fingers denotes that your love will be requited and that you will become renowned for your benevolence. To see well kept nails indicates scholarly tastes and literary success.

fire

Fire is favorable to the dreamer if he does not get burned. To dream that your home is burning denotes a loving companion, obedient children, and careful servants. To dream that a store is burning foretells a great rush in business and profitable results.

frogs

To see frogs in a
dream signifies that
you will have a
pleasant and even-
tempered friend
as your confidant
and counselor.

gloves

To dream of wearing new gloves denotes that you will be cautious and economical in your dealings with others. You will have lawsuits or business troubles, but you will settle them in a manner that satisfies you. To find a pair of gloves denotes a marriage or new love affair.

goblet

To see goblets of ancient design means that you will receive favors and benefits from strangers. For a woman to give a man a glass goblet full of water denotes illicit pleasures.

grapes

If you see grapes growing in abundance among leaves, you will soon attain eminent positions and be able to impart happiness to others. For a young woman this dream is one of bright promise. She will have her most ardent wish granted.

grass

This is a very fortunate dream indeed. It gives a promise of a happy and well advanced life to the tradesman, rapid accumulation of wealth, fame to artistic and literary people, and a safe voyage through the turbulent sea of love.

hat

For a man to dream that he wears a new hat predicts a change of place and business which will be very much to his advantage. For a woman to dream that she wears a fine new hat denotes the attainment of wealth and that she will be the object of much admiration. For the wind to blow off your hat denotes a sudden change in affairs.

hens

To dream of hens
predicts pleasant
family reunions with
added members.

honey

To dream of eating
honey foretells
that you will attain
wealth and love.
To lovers this indi-
cates a swift rush
into marital joys.

horse

If you dream of seeing or riding a white horse, it is an indication of prosperity and pleasurable commingling with friends. To dream of dark horses signifies prosperous conditions but a large amount of discontent.

house

If you dream of building a house, you will make wise changes in your present affairs. To dream that you own an elegant house denotes that you will soon leave your home for a better one and that fortune will be kind to you.

ice cream

To dream that you are eating ice cream foretells happy success in affairs already undertaken. To see children eating it predicts that prosperity and happiness will attend you most favorably.

island

To see an island is symbolic of comfort and easy circumstances after much striving and worrying to meet honorable obligations. To see people on an island denotes a struggle to raise yourself higher in prominent circles.

ivy

To dream of seeing ivy growing on trees or houses predicts excellent health and an increase of fortune. Innumerable joys will succeed this dream. To a young woman ivy means many prized distinctions. If she sees it clinging to the wall in the moonlight, she will have clandestine meetings with young men.

jewels

To dream of jewels denotes much pleasure and riches. To wear them brings rank and satisfied ambitions. If you see others wearing them, distinguished places will be held by you or some friend.

jockey

To dream of a jockey is an omen that you will appreciate a gift from an unexpected source. For a young woman to dream that she associates with a jockey, or has one for a lover, indicates that she will win a husband out of her station. To see a jockey thrown from a horse signifies that strangers will call upon you for aid.

jury

To dream that you are on a jury denotes dissatisfaction with your employment and that you will seek to change your position. If you are cleared from a charge by a jury, your business will be successful and affairs will move your way but if you should be condemned, enemies will over-power you and harass you beyond endurance.

kangaroo

To see a kangaroo
in your dreams
means that you will
outwit a wily enemy
who seeks to place
you in an unfavorable
position before
the public.

key

To dream of keys denotes unexpected change. If the keys are lost, unpleasant adventures will affect you. To find keys brings domestic peace and brisk turns to business.

kiss

To see children kissing means that happy reunions in families and satisfactory work will follow. To dream that you kiss your mother predicts that you will be very successful in your enterprises and be honored and beloved by your friends. To kiss your sweetheart in the dark denotes dangers and immoral engagements. To kiss her in the light signifies honorable intentions.

lace

If a woman dreams of lace, she will be happy in the realization of her most ambitious desires and lovers will bow to her command without questioning.

ladder

To dream of a ladder being raised for you to ascend predicts that energetic and nervy qualifications will raise you to prominence in business affairs. To ascend a ladder means prosperity and uninterrupted happiness.

lamb

To dream of lambs frolicking in green pastures signifies chaste friendships and joys, bounteous and profitable crops to farmers, and increase of possessions for others. A lost lamb means that wayward people will be under your influence.

letters

To dream often
of receiving a letter
from a friend fore-
tells their arrival
or that you will hear
from them by letter
or otherwise.

lion

To dream of a lion signifies that a great force is driving you. If you subdue the lion, you will be victorious in any engagement. If it overpowers you, you will be open to the successful attacks of enemies.

money

To dream of finding
money denotes small
worries but much
happiness. Changes
will follow.

moon

To dream of seeing the moon with
the aspect of the heavens remaining
normal is an omen of success in love
and business affairs. To see the new
moon denotes an increase in wealth
and congenial partners in marriage.

mountain

If you ascend a mountain in your dreams and the way is pleasant and verdant, you will rise to wealth and prominence. If the mountain is rugged and you fail to reach the top, you may expect reverses in your life. To awaken when you are at a dangerous point in ascending indicates that you will find affairs taking a flattering turn.

music

To dream of hearing
harmonious music
is an omen of pleasure
and prosperity.
Discordant music
foretells troubles with
unruly children.

naked

To dream that you suddenly discover your nudity and are trying to conceal it denotes that you have sought illicit pleasure, contrary to your noblest instincts, and are desirous of abandoning those desires.

needle

To find a needle
predicts that you will
have friends who
appreciate you.
To look for a needle
foretells useless
worries.

nightingale

To dream that you are listening to the pleasant notes of the nightingale signifies a pleasing existence and prosperous and healthy surroundings. This is a most favorable dream to lovers and parents.

nose

To see your own nose indicates force of character and consciousness of your ability to accomplish whatever enterprise you may choose to undertake.

nurse

To see a nurse leaving your house is an omen of good health in the family. For a young woman to dream that she is a nurse means that she will gain the esteem of people through her self-sacrifice.

oatmeal

To dream of eating oatmeal signifies the enjoyment of worthily earned fortune. For a young woman to dream of preparing it for the table means that she will soon preside over the destiny of others.

oceans

It is hopeful to dream of the ocean when it is calm. The sailor will have a pleasant and profitable voyage, those in business will enjoy a season of remuneration, and the young man will revel in his sweetheart's charms.

onions

If you eat onions in a dream, you will overcome all opposition. If you see them growing, there will be just enough rivalry in your affairs to make things interesting.

organ

To hear the pealing forth of an organ in grand anthems signifies lasting friendships and well-grounded fortune. If you dream of rendering harmonious music on an organ you will be fortunate in the way of worldly comfort and much social distinction will be given you.

palm tree

Palm trees seen in your dreams are messages of hopeful situations and happiness of a high order.

park

To dream of walking through a well-kept park denotes enjoyable leisure. If you walk with your lover, you will be comfortably and happily married.

pearls

To dream of pearls is a forerunner of good business, trade, and affairs of social nature. If a young woman dreams that her lover sends her gifts of pearls, she will indeed be most fortunate. There will be occasions of festivity and pleasure for her, along with a loving and faithful engagement without the jealous inclinations so ruinous to the peace of lovers.

pig

To dream of
a fat, healthy pig
indicates rea-
sonable success
in affairs.

potatoes

Dreaming of potatoes brings incidents of good. To dream of digging them denotes success. To dream of eating them means that you will enjoy substantial gain. To cook them foretells pleasant employment. Planting potatoes brings realization of desires.

quaker

To dream of a Quaker denotes that you will have faithful friends and fair business. If you dream that you are a Quaker, you will deport yourself honorably toward an enemy.

queen

To dream of a queen foretells successful ventures. If she looks old or haggard, there will be disappointments connected with your pleasures.

quilts

To dream of quilts foretells pleasant
and comfortable circumstances. For a
young woman, this dream foretells that
her practical, wise, business-like ways
will advance her into favorable esteem.

rabbits

To dream of rabbits foretells a favorable turn in conditions. You will be more pleased with your gains than you were formerly. To see white rabbits signifies faithfulness in love to the married or single. To see rabbits frolicking about denotes that children will contribute to your joys.

rainbow

To see a rainbow in a dream predicts unusual happenings. Affairs will assume a more promising countenance and crops will give promise of a plentiful yield. For lovers to see the rainbow is an omen of much happiness in their union. To see the rainbow hanging low over green trees signifies unconditional success in any undertaking.

reindeer

To dream of a reindeer signifies faithful duty and loyalty to friends.

roses

To dream of seeing roses blooming and fragrant denotes that some joyful occasion is nearing and you will possess the faithful love of your sweetheart. To inhale their fragrance brings unalloyed pleasure.

slippers

To dream that your slippers are much admired foretells that you will be involved in a flirtation that will bring disgrace.

soap

To dream of soap foretells that friendships will reveal interesting entertainment. Farmers will have success in their varied affairs. For a young woman to be making soap is an omen that a substantial and satisfactory competency will be hers.

squirrel

To dream of seeing squirrels means that pleasant friends will soon visit you. You will also see advancement in your business. To pet one signifies family joy.

stars

To dream of looking upon clear, shining stars foretells good health and prosperity. If you dream of stars appearing and vanishing mysteriously, there will be some strange changes and happenings in your near future.

sun

To dream of seeing a clear, shining sunrise signifies joyous events and prosperity. To see the sun at noontide denotes the maturity of ambitions and signals unbounded satisfaction. A sun shining through clouds indicates that troubles and difficulties are losing their hold on you and that prosperity is nearing.

swans

To dream of seeing white swans floating upon placid waters foretells prosperous outlooks and delightful experiences. To see a black swan denotes illicit pleasure.

tea

To dream that you
are thirsty for tea
means that you will
be surprised with
uninvited guests.

theater

To dream of being at a theater prophesizes that you will have much pleasure in the company of new friends. Your affairs will be satisfactory after this dream. If you are one of the players, your pleasures will be of short duration.

tomatoes

To dream of eating tomatoes signals the approach of good health. To see them growing denotes domestic enjoyment and happiness. For a young woman to see a ripe tomato foretells her happiness in the married state.

turtle

To dream of seeing turtles signifies that an unusual incident will bring you enjoyment and improve your business conditions. To drink turtle soup denotes that you will find pleasure in compromising intrigue.

tower

To dream of seeing
a tower denotes
that you will aspire
to high elevations.
If you climb one
you will succeed in
your wishes.

umbrella

To carry a new umbrella over you in a clear shower or sunshine is an omen of exquisite pleasure and prosperity. To see others carrying them foretells that you will be appealed to for aid by charity.

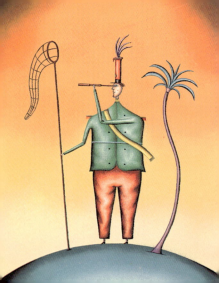

uniform

To see a uniform in your dream means
that you will have influential friends to
aid you in obtaining your desires.

vegetables

To dream of eating vegetables is an omen of strange luck.

veil

To dream that you wear a veil foretells that you will not be perfectly
sincere with your lover and will be
forced to use trickery to retain him.

vineyard

To dream of a vine-
yard denotes favorable
investments and auspi-
cious love-making.

violets

To see violets
in your dreams, or
gather them, brings
joyous occasions
in which you will
find favor with some
superior person.

violin

To see or hear a violin in dreams foretells harmony and peace in the family and that financial affairs will cause no apprehension. For a young woman to play one in her dreams signifies that she will be honored and receive lavish gifts.

waltz

To see the waltz danced suggests that you will have pleasant relations with a cheerful and adventuresome person. If a woman waltzes with another woman, she will be loved for her virtues. If she sees persons whirling in the waltz as if intoxicated, she will be engulfed so deeply in desire and pleasure that it will be a miracle if she resists the impassioned advances of her lover.

water

To play in the water denotes a sudden awakening to love and passion. To have it sprayed on your head denotes that your passionate awakening to love will meet reciprocal consummation.

waterfall

To dream of a waterfall foretells that you will secure your wildest desire and that fortune will be exceedingly favorable to your progress.

waves

To dream of waves
is a sign that you hold
some vital step in
contemplation; if the
waves are clear,
that step will result in
much knowledge.

wine

To dream of drinking wine predicts joy and consequent friendships. To dream of breaking bottles of wine foretells that your love and passion will border on excess. To see barrels of wine is symbolic of great luxury. To pour it from one vessel into another signifies that your enjoyments will be varied and that you will journey to many notable places.

yarn

To dream of
yarn denotes
success in
business and
an industrious
companion in
your home.

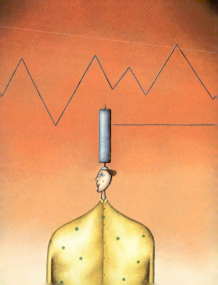

zebra

To dream of a zebra predicts that you will be interested in varying and fleeting enterprises.

zodiac

To study the zodiac in your dreams means that you will gain distinction and favor through your intercourse with strangers. If you approach it or it approaches you, you will succeed in your endeavors to the wonderment of others and beyond your wildest imagination. To draw a map of it signifies future gain.

This book is bound using handcraft methods, and is Smyth-sewn to ensure durability.

The book was illustrated by Haydn Cornner.

The book was designed by Frances J. Soo Ping Chow.

The text was edited by Jenny Comita.

The text was set in Americana and Gill Sans.

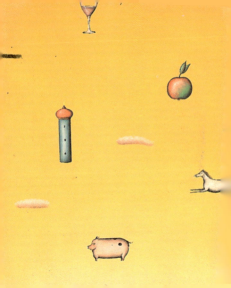